Gardeners' World

POCKET PLANTS

WINTER COLOUR

Andi Cleevely

Photographs by Jo Whitworth

BBC Books

Published by BBC Books,
an imprint of BBC Worldwide Publishing,
BBC Worldwide Limited, Woodlands,
80 Wood Lane, London W12 0TT

First published 1997
© BBC Worldwide Limited 1997
The moral right of the author has been asserted

ISBN 0 563 38372 0

Photographs by Jo Whitworth

Artwork by Pond and Giles

Set in Futura

Printed and bound in Belgium by Proost NV
Colour separations by Radstock Reproductions, Midsomer Norton, Avon
Cover printed in Belgium by Proost NV

Author Biography

Andi Clevely has been a working gardener for nearly thirty years. He began his career in Leeds City Council central nurseries and since then has worked in many gardens around the country, including Windsor Great Park. He is now responsible for a country estate and large garden in Stratford-on-Avon where he lives with his family. Andi has written a number of gardening books and is a regular columnist for *Homes & Gardens* magazine.

Acknowledgements

The publishers would like to thank The Sir Harold Hillier Gardens and Arboretum, Ampfield near Romsey, Hampshire and The Royal Horticultural Society Gardens, Wisley, Surrey for their assistance with the photography. All photographs © BBC.

Planning the Winter Garden

 Flowers

 Foliage

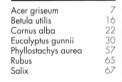 Bark

 Fruits

 Ericaceous

INTRODUCTION

There is a special magic and sharpened simplicity about the colours and shapes that come into their own in winter. As this book reveals, a wide range of easily grown plants – from trees and shrubs to dwarf bulbs and tiny succulents – is available to provide attractive (and often fragrant) flowers, startling leaf and bark colours, or vivid berries and other fruits that will illuminate the short days of winter twilight.

Planning

Where possible it is a good idea to reconsider a garden's overall appearance in winter. Once leaves have been shed and seasonal plants have died down, its complete shape and the arrangement of plants is much clearer.

Then is the time to assess whether growing a few carefully sited evergreen shrubs, perhaps varieties with bright variegated leaves, or deciduous species with red or gold stems might provide colour and form in otherwise empty beds. Add some winter flowers as companion plants to make imaginative combinations – a red dogwood with variegated euonymus, for example, or a mixture of dwarf daffodils and hellebores.

Even the brown dormant stems of some grasses can look charming when edged with frost and underplanted with drifts of winter aconites and hardy cyclamen. Do not be afraid to experiment: there is less risk of making mistakes at a season when any colour is welcome.

Growing conditions

Careful planning and preparation will help plants withstand the sometimes savage weather of winter.

Position: Light is at a premium in winter. Some species need all they can get, while others are content in varying degrees of shade. It is important to position plants where they grow best, but also where you can see them to advantage: variegated evergreens rarely colour well in shade, for example, but they will glow with startling brilliance planted in full sun and show up well against a dark green background.

Shelter: Strong wind can break brittle stems and scorch foliage, so position vulnerable plants where they are sheltered by tougher plants, or by a hedge, fence or wall, which may also offer them a little more welcome warmth. Shelter can also advance growth and flowering, coaxing some early spring species to bloom in late winter.

Drainage: Soils may become cold and wet, even waterlogged in winter, creating conditions in which roots cannot survive. The correct preparation of the ground will often remedy this, but it is sometimes best to build a raised bed or grow susceptible plants in containers.

Preparing the ground

With the exception of plants such as bulbs and corms that may be planted straight into grass, the site needs to be dug or forked over thoroughly in advance of planting. Remove all weeds, especially perennial kinds, and then where necessary improve the soil according to its type.

Heavy soils: These are the kind likely to be cold and waterlogged in a wet season, so dig in plenty of grit or fine gravel to open up the structure and assist drainage.

Keeping the surface covered with a mulch of coarse material such as shredded bark helps prevent the surface from becoming greasy and compacted by rain.

Light soils: These normally drain well, sometimes too freely, and the addition of moisture-retentive materials is necessary to prevent roots from drying out later in the year. Fork in plenty of organic matter such as garden compost, leaf mould, composted bark or well-rotted manure before planting. Mulching will stop the soil from drying out.

Planting

Container-grown plants may be planted at any time when the soil is not too wet or frozen. Bare-rooted shrubs, trees and other plants are normally planted while they are dormant, preferably in autumn but any time between then and early spring; evergreens are planted in mid-autumn or mid-spring. Optimum times are given in the individual entries.

The same simple planting procedure applies to most species.

- Prepare the site thoroughly beforehand, preferably a few weeks earlier.

- Arrange plants on the surface first to check their positioning; then dig out a hole for each one, large enough to accommodate the roots comfortably and at the same depth as the plant was previously growing.

- Break up the excavated soil, add any fertilizer, and replace around the plant and firm gently into place. Water in well if planting during a dry spell, and mulch where recommended.

- Trees should be provided with supporting stakes driven into the hole before planting and secured to the main stem with cushioned tree ties.

- Bulbs are planted into soil prepared as above or direct into turf, using a trowel or proprietary bulb planter.

Care

Watering: This is rarely necessary, except when planting during a dry autumn. Plants growing in containers should be checked regularly, because the roots can dry out quickly in windy conditions; take care not to over-water, and insulate containers against frost: even when moist, plants can die from dehydration if the rootball is frozen.

Feeding: Supplementary feeding is seldom needed solely for winter performance, but it may be important at planting time for long-term sustenance and also in late winter to fuel new growth as conditions improve. Container plants actively growing in winter should be fed occasionally with a balanced fertilizer.

Pruning: In most cases this is done after flowering or when new growth is about to appear. Some plants flourish without routine pruning, apart from removing dead and damaged material, while others need regular attention to lay the foundation for success the following winter: check details in the individual entries.

Propagation: Perennial is a relative description, and plants age at a varying rate, their performance sometimes suffering as they get older or become overgrown. Mature herbaceous perennials and clumps of bulbs can be divided (split into smaller portions) after a few years to restore their vigour; most ageing shrubs can be propagated by various means to provide young replacements with greater vitality.

And finally ...

Plant winter species generously: the flowers, stems or foliage of most kinds can be cut for indoor decoration, which is always appreciated during the darker months of winter, so make sure that you have plenty to spare.

Abeliophyllum distichum White Forsythia

ABELIOPHYLLUM DISTICHUM

This unusual late-winter flowering shrub makes a good alternative to, or companion for, forsythia, a close relative. The white starry blooms are fragrant and last well indoors in water. Young plants look very wispy and frail, but they are quite tough and slowly develop into robust bushes.

Plant type: Deciduous shrub.

Height: 1.5m (5ft).

Spread: 1.2m (4ft).

Soil: Any ordinary soil.

Positioning: Full sun or light shade with shelter from cold winds; free-standing bush in beds, borders and shrubberies, or trained on a dark-coloured wall. Site behind herbaceous flowers for later interest.

Planting time: Autumn or spring.

Care: Mulch with compost after spring pruning. Evenly fan out and tie developing branches of wall-trained plants on wires or trellis. Remove up to one-third of the oldest branches annually from mature plants.

Propagation: Grow cuttings in a cold frame in summer, outdoors in autumn.

Recommended: Normal species; also Roseum Group (pink-flushed flowers).

Useful tip: Protect early blooms from hard frosts by training on a warm wall or fence; trained plants can reach 2.5m (8ft) high and wide.

Related plants: None.

Acer griseum
Paperbark Maple

ACER GRISEUM

Plant type: Deciduous small tree.
Height: 6m (20ft) or more.
Spread: 4m (13ft).
Soil: Rich; moist but well-drained.
Positioning: Full sun or very light shade, sheltered from the strongest winds. Best grown prominently in lawns or shrubberies to appreciate the full beauty of the bark.
Planting time: Autumn to spring, while trees are dormant.
Care: Stake trees for the first few years and mulch in spring with compost. No routine pruning. Watch out for aphids on young leaves and spray with insecticide.
Propagation: Sow seeds in autumn; expose to frost before moving to a cold frame in spring.
Recommended: Normal species only.
Useful tip: Buy a tree in autumn when you can select the best leaf colour.
Related plants: A. grosseri var. hersii (marbled white bark); A. palmatum 'Sango-kaku' (coral-pink bark); A. pensylvanicum 'Erythrocladum' (salmon-pink bark with white markings).

One of the loveliest of all small garden trees, Acer is eye-catching at every season, with yellow flower clusters in spring; trios of leaves that emerge pink or bronze, then turn green and finally crimson in autumn; and warm copper-brown bark that peels like parchment in winter.

ADONIS AMURENSIS 'FUKUJUKAI'

These are choice early perennials, with flowers like superior 5cm (2in) diameter buttercups. The first blooms often emerge at the turn of the year in sheltered corners. The finely cut leaves that follow soon afterwards form a charming nest for the bright flowers and last well into summer. A good choice for cold gardens, where the colour of the blooms is often more intense.

Plant type: Herbaceous perennial.
Height: 20–45cm (8–18in).
Spread: 30cm (12in).
Soil: Most moist, fertile soils.
Positioning: Full sun or very light shade, with some shelter from late winter winds. Effective in clumps or drifts at the front of borders, in rock gardens, especially if grown with cowslips.
Planting time: Autumn or spring.
Care: Plant 15–20cm (6–8in) apart. Mulch with compost after planting and annually after flowering.
Propagation: Divide clumps in spring; sow ripe seeds in a cold frame (germination can be very slow).
Recommended: *A. amurensis* (large golden blooms, double in the form 'Flore Pleno'); 'Fukujukai' (glistening yellow with purple young leaves); *A. vernalis* (large single flowers, bright yellow but occasionally white).
Useful tip: Grow well away from invasive perennials like bugle and Lamium.
Related plants: None.

Ajuga reptans Bugle, Carpenter's Herb

Plant type: Evergreen creeping perennial.
Height: 15cm (6in).
Spread: 30cm (12in).
Soil: Any reasonable soil, preferably moist and fertile.
Positioning: Dappled sunlight or moist shade. Ideal for carpeting banks, under hedges, at the front of borders, especially associated with dwarf grasses and spring bulbs; also for crevices in rocks and paving and as ground cover in herb gardens.
Planting time: Autumn or spring.
Care: Water in dry seasons. If necessary limit spread by division every 3–4 years.
Propagation: Divide in autumn or spring.
Recommended: *A. reptans*, especially variegated forms 'Atropurpurea', 'Burgundy Glow', 'Multicolor' (syns. 'Rainbow', 'Tricolor') for shade only.
Useful tip: Dark-leafed varieties are best in open sunny positions; grow paler multicoloured ones in light shade.
Related plants: *A. pyramidalis*.

AJUGA REPTANS 'CATLINS GIANT'

The dense spikes of blue (sometimes white) spring flowers are charming, but bugle's outstanding decorative feature is its dense mats of variously coloured foliage which often glow in the winter sunshine. This is a versatile plant for a number of challenging positions, since there is little that will deter the strong rooting stems from spreading heartily to weave a solid mat of prostrate foliage.

9

ANEMONE BLANDA

The mountain anemones of Greece appear with the snowdrops, first as solitary blooms wherever the sun is warmest. Plants very soon develop into startling drifts of deep blue daisies that sway in the lightest breeze, after which all growth fades away very quickly. There are many colour forms, although the basic species is perhaps the most charming.

Plant type:	Herbaceous rhizomatous perennial.
Height:	10cm (4in).
Spread:	5cm (2in).
Soil:	Light, free-draining; some leafy humus.
Positioning:	Full sun or light shade; in large groups and drifts on banks, under shrubs and trees; also in rock gardens or between paving slabs. Combine with winter aconites, snowdrops and dwarf cyclamen.
Planting time:	Early autumn.
Care:	Plant 8cm (3in) deep and 5cm (2in) apart in generous groups. Mulch with leaf mould or compost in autumn.
Propagation:	Divide large clumps in late summer; replant immediately.
Recommended:	Normal blue species; also named selections, such as 'Charmer', rosy red; 'Ingramii' (syn. 'Atrocaerulea'), deep blue; 'Radar', magenta and white; var. *rosea*, pale pink; 'White Splendour'.
Useful tip:	Plants self-seed freely in corners and crevices.
Related plants:	Attractive species such as *A. appenina* tend to appear after winter.

Artemisia Wormwood

Plant type: Evergreen shrub.
Height: 90cm–1.2m (3–4ft).
Spread: 60–90cm (2–3ft).
Soil: Light, dry, well-drained; preferably alkaline.
Positioning: Warm, sheltered from winds. Grow on dry banks, below warm walls, in rock and herb gardens; also in containers. Very pretty with small bulbs like winter aconites and *Anemone blanda*.
Planting time: Mid- to late spring.
Care: Mulch with grit or gravel after planting. Protect in winter with fleece or fine netting. Trim back frost damage in spring.
Propagation: Grow cuttings in a cold frame or under glass in summer.
Recommended: Normal species; 'Faith Raven' and 'Brass Band' (now *A.* 'Powis Castle') are slightly hardier forms.
Useful tip: If winters are regularly cold and damp grow plants in containers; move under cover or into warm shelter in early winter.
Related plants: *A. absinthium* 'Lambrook Giant'.

ARTEMISIA LUDOVICIANA 'SILVER QUEEN'

This showy silver shrub is a native of sandy and rocky Mediterranean shores, and needs perfect drainage in poor dry soils if it is to survive average winters unscathed. It is worth special care, for its silky foliage is the finest of all the artemisias.

SSP. *ITALICUM* 'MARMORATUM'

Several hardy arums send up arrow-shaped young leaves at the start of winter. These look fresh and elegant throughout the coldest months, and eventually fade away in early summer, together with the typical furled arum flower. The variegated forms of this woodland plant are particularly desirable.

Plant type: Herbaceous tuberous perennial.
Height: 45cm (18in).
Spread: 30cm (12in).
Soil: Fertile, moisture-retentive.
Positioning: Full sun for the brightest winter colour, with some shade in early summer. Grow at the base of hedges and beneath trees, with snowdrops, hellebores and *Iris foetidissima*.
Planting time: Late summer.
Care: Plant tubers 10cm (4in) deep and 23cm (9in) apart in groups. Mulch with compost or leaf mould in autumn.
Propagation: Divide in late summer.
Recommended: Normal plain green species; also ssp. *italicum* 'Marmoratum' (leaves marbled grey and cream), 'Chameleon' (yellow marbling), 'Tiny' (cream markings, dwarf), 'White Winter' (bold white markings).
Useful tip: The bright red berries that appear in autumn are poisonous.
Related plants: *A. creticum*, *A. orientale* and *A. dioscoridis*.

Aucuba japonica Spotted Laurel

Plant type: Evergreen shrub.

Height: 2.4–3.6m (8–12ft).

Spread: 3m (10ft).

Soil: Most kinds unless waterlogged.

Positioning: Full shade (green varieties) or semi-shade (variegated kinds). Grow as specimens in borders or large containers. Plant 90cm (3ft) apart for hedges and windbreaks.

Planting time: Autumn or mid-spring.

Care: Leave unpruned, or trim in mid-spring. Clip hedges in mid-summer.

Propagation: Grow cuttings in a cold frame in summer, outdoors in autumn.

Recommended: 'Crotonifolia' (golden mottling, female), 'Gold Dust' (speckled with yellow, female), 'Longifolia' (slim green leaves, female), 'Picturata' (central yellow blotches, male), 'Rozannie' (bisexual with good red berries), 'Variegata', syn. 'Maculata' (large yellow spots, female).

Useful tip: Cut leaves turn brown, so trim with secateurs.

Related plants: None.

AUCUBA JAPONICA 'PICTURATA'

These handsome plants survive in a wide range of sites, and easily tolerate urban pollution, seaside exposure, dry soils or competition from conifers. Their evergreen leaves, often with bright variegation, and the berries borne by females, make them valuable winter plants.

BERBERIS LINEARIFOLIA 'JEWEL'

Unlike the deciduous berberis, which are noted for their autumn foliar tints, evergreen varieties provide outstanding year-round interest. They are spiny spring-flowering shrubs, with attractive autumn berries and dense foliage in a range of shapes and shades of rich glossy green.

Plant type:	Evergreen shrub.
Height:	3m (10ft).
Spread:	Up to 3m (10ft).
Soil:	Preferably fertile, rich in humus, but most kinds if not waterlogged.
Positioning:	Full sun for spring flowers; light shade is tolerated. Ideal for shady corners, exposed positions, heavy soil. Withstands urban pollution.
Planting time:	Early autumn or mid-spring; bare-root plants spring only.
Care:	Trim lightly to shape after flowering; hard prune overgrown plants in mid-spring.
Propagation:	Grow cuttings in a cold frame in summer, outdoors in autumn.
Recommended:	B. 'Goldilocks' (deep gold flowers on red stalks); B. linearifolia 'Jewel' (scarlet buds, orange flowers); B. × stenophylla 'Crawley Gem' (orange), 'Irwinii' (deep yellow), 'Corallina Compacta' (yellow, dwarf), 'Claret Cascade' (red-orange).
Useful tip:	Plant 75cm (30in) apart for a hedge.
Related plants:	None.

Bergenia Elephant's Ears

Plant type: Evergreen perennial.
Height: 30–45cm (12–18in).
Spread: 45–60cm (18–24in).
Soil: Most kinds, including dry impoverished soils.
Positioning: Full sun or shade; as ground cover, edging and compact foliage plants in beds and borders. Plant 30cm (12in) apart in groups. Combine with *Brunnera* and *Omphalodes*.
Planting time: Autumn or spring.
Care: Mulch with compost in late winter; remove dead or injured leaves in early spring. Divide every 4–5 years.
Propagation: Divide in autumn or after spring flowering.
Recommended: *B. cordifolia* 'Purpurea' (purple-edged leaves, rose-pink flowers); *B. × schmidtii* (frilled leaves, pink flowers); *B.* 'Abendglut' (mahogany foliage, red flowers); *B.* 'Silberlicht' (white flowers).
Useful tip: Plants are ideal for windy positions, sites near water.
Related plants: Several saxifrages are ideal for winter colour (see Saxifraga).

BERGENIA × SCHMIDTII

These bold large-leafed plants thrive in the most demanding positions and offer all-year-round foliage. Large dense heads of blooms sometimes appear in late winter. The solid clumps are excellent as edging when spilling over the sides of paths.

15

Betula utilis Himalayan Birch

BETULA UTILIS VAR. JACQUEMONTII 'JERMYNS'

Winter emphasizes the graceful form and startling white bark of these light, elegant trees and they are ideal choices for providing dappled shade and outstanding autumn leaf tints. They may be pruned to size for smaller gardens.

Plant type: Deciduous tree.

Height: 9m (30ft).

Spread: 1.5m (5ft).

Soil: Most kinds unless shallow chalk or waterlogged.

Positioning: Full sun or light shade; as a specimen on lawns, at the edge of woodland or against an evergreen background. Plant several 45–60cm (18–24in) apart for a multi-stemmed clump. Underplant with bulbs and evergreen ground cover like bergenias.

Planting time: Between autumn and spring, while dormant.

Care: Stake for the first few years. Prune leading shoots in winter to make shorter bushy trees if necessary.

Propagation: Sow species seeds in autumn, exposed to frost; graft varieties on *B. pendula* rootstocks in spring.

Recommended: var. *jacquemontii* (syn. *B. jacquemontii*) 'Silver Shadow', 'Doorenbos'.

Useful tip: Scrub trunks with warm soapy water to enhance colouring and kill algae.

Related plants: *B. nigra*.

Plant type: Biennial.

Height: 23–45cm (9–18in).

Spread: 30–45cm (12–18in).

Soil: Moist, well-drained; a little lime.

Positioning: Full sun for the best colouring; or very light shade. Plant 30–45cm (12–18in) apart in groups. Grow in beds, borders, containers.

Planting time: Early autumn.

Care: Remove discoloured leaves after wet spells; cover when a hard frost is forecast.

Propagation: Sow seeds under glass in mid-summer; prick out into small pots and grow in a cold frame.

Recommended: B. oleracea Capitata Group and B. o. Acephala Group are sold as mixtures, and sometimes ('Red Osaka', 'White Peacock') as single colours.

Useful tip: Sow a second batch a month after the first to replace winter losses. Plants will flower in spring and set seed (mixed if several colours are grown together).

Related plants: None.

BRASSICA OLERACEA 'RAGGED JACK'

Flowering cabbage and the taller kale varieties have been popular for many years in the Far East as autumn and winter bedding. They develop large heads with brightly coloured hearts in shades of red, purple, pink and white. As temperatures drop below 10°C (50°F), colours become more vivid.

CALLUNA VULGARIS 'JULIA'

The foliage of summer- and autumn-flowering Callunas makes them essential for winter gardens. Coloured forms are dense compact plants, with tiny overlapping leaves that often erupt in shades of gold, flame and orange as the season turns cold.

Plant type: Evergreen shrub.

Height: 20–45cm (8–18in).

Spread: Up to 90cm (3ft).

Soil: Moist, well-drained; fairly light, rich in humus; acid.

Positioning: Full sun for the best foliage colour; some flowering varieties tolerate light shade. Plant 30–40cm (12–15in) apart as edging or in groups for ground cover; superb specimens in rock gardens, containers.

Planting time: Spring or autumn.

Care: Plant with the lowest branches on the surface, then mulch with composted bark. Trim annually after flowering.

Propagation: Grow cuttings in a cold frame in spring or early summer.

Recommended: Gold/red foliage: 'Sir John Charrington', 'Golden Carpet', 'Beoley Gold', 'Wickwar Flame'. Silver/grey foliage: 'Silver Knight', 'Silver Queen'.

Useful tip: Make a raised bed if a site is waterlogged.

Related plants: *Daboecia* and *Erica* varieties.

Camellia Camellia

Plant type: Evergreen shrub or small tree.

Height: 1.8–3m (6–10ft).

Spread: 1.8–3m (6–10ft).

Soil: Moist, well-drained; acid.

Positioning: Light shade in mild gardens, otherwise full sun with shelter from frost, cold dry winds; try to shield from early morning sun. Grow as a wall shrub or specimen in a large container.

Planting time: Spring.

Care: Feed and mulch with compost after pruning to shape in spring. Water with rainwater, especially as buds form. Deadhead.

Propagation: Layer in early spring.

Recommended: C. japonica 'Berenice Boddy' (light pink), 'Elegans' (deep pink); C. sasanqua 'Crimson King' (red), 'Narumi-gata' (white, pink tips); C. x williamsii 'Debbie' (rose pink), 'Leonard Messel' (apricot pink), 'St Ewe' (rose pink).

Useful tip: Grow C. sasanqua in a conservatory in cold districts.

Related plants: Many other species.

CAMELLIA JAPONICA 'PINK PERFECTION'

Camellias are wonderful winter shrubs with dark, glossy evergreen leaves. They are perfectly hardy and it is often the lustrous blooms that need protection from frost – depending on situation, they can appear any time between early winter and early spring. Grow in the shelter of a warm wall for perfect flowers.

CAREX TESTACEA

Sedges look pretty wherever they are grown in the garden. They make non-invasive clumps of fine narrow leaves that are almost evergreen, and change colour subtly as the year progresses, remaining graceful all winter. The delicate male and female flowers appear in summer.

Plant type: Evergreen or semi-evergreen grass-like perennial.

Height: 45–90cm (18–36in).

Spread: 45–60cm (18–24in).

Soil: Moist, but not water-logged; a few species prefer dry soil.

Positioning: Full sun or light shade. Ideal as a marginal pond plant and in bog gardens; also at the front of borders with grasses, heathers.

Planting time: Autumn or spring.

Care: Feed with general fertilizer in spring; mulch in autumn with compost or decayed leaves. Cut down old top growth in spring. Divide plants every 5–6 years and replant in fresh soil.

Propagation: Divide in autumn or spring.

Recommended: C. buchananii (Fox-red Sedge), prefers dry soils; C. firma 'Variegata' (Dwarf Pillow Sedge), compact; C. testacea; C. hachijoensis 'Evergold'.

Useful tip: Leave plenty of room for the arching foliage to fall on all sides.

Related plants: None.

Clematis cirrhosa Fern-leafed Clematis

Plant type: Evergreen climber.
Height: Up to 5–6m (16–19ft).
Spread: 2–3m (6½–10ft).
Soil: Fertile, free-draining.
Positioning: In a conservatory or on a warm sheltered wall in cold districts; on a slightly shaded wall in very favoured gardens. In a container or raised bed if the soil is heavy.
Planting time: Spring.
Care: Mulch after flowering with garden compost or composted bark; feed container plants every fortnight during flowering. Prune after flowering by cutting back side-shoots close to their base and just beyond a leaf joint. Cut all top growth back to the same point each year if space is limited
Propagation: Grow cuttings under glass in summer.
Recommended: Basic species; also var. *balearica* (speckled flowers); 'Freckles' (large flowers); 'Wisley Cream'.
Useful tip: Watch out for greenfly and other insect pests if grown under glass.
Related plants: *C. napaulensis.*

CLEMATIS CIRRHOSA 'FRECKLES'

These elegant evergreen climbers bear fragrant bell-shaped blooms, up to 5cm (2in) across, that may be clear cream in colour or variably speckled with maroon according to variety. The leaves are plain or finely cut, and often tinted with purple in winter. An altogether choice plant for a special position.

Cornus alba Red-barked Dogwood

CORNUS ALBA 'SIBIRICA'

If left unpruned, these dogwoods soon make large branching thickets. Regular pruning, however, keeps them at a manageable size and stimulates the growth of brightly coloured new stems. Varieties with variegated leaves are interesting throughout the year.

Plant type: Deciduous shrub.
Height: Species 3m (10ft), varieties 2m (6½ft).
Spread: 1.8–2.4m (6–8ft).
Soil: Most kinds.
Positioning: Full sun or light shade; singly in borders with grasses and evergreen shrubs, beside water. Dramatic in groups of three or more.
Planting time: Autumn or spring.
Care: In early spring prune almost to ground level, chop out suckers with a spade. Feed after pruning and mulch with compost.
Propagation: Grow cuttings under glass in summer, outdoors in autumn.
Recommended: Normal species; also 'Elegantissima' (red stems, white variegated leaves), 'Kesselringii' (deep purple stems, young foliage red), 'Sibirica' (crimson stems, green leaves), 'Spaethii' (red stems, gold leaves).
Useful tip: Cut back green-leafed forms completely every two years; shorten the stems of coloured ones by one-third annually.
Related plants: *C. stolonifera* 'Flaviramea'.

Plant type:	Deciduous corm.
Height:	8–13cm (3–5in).
Spread:	10cm (4in).
Soil:	Any well-drained soil.
Positioning:	Full sun or light shade; naturalize in groups and drifts in grass. Plant under trees and shrubs, also in rock gardens, borders and containers.
Planting time:	Early to late autumn.
Care:	Plant 8cm (3in) deep and 8–10cm (3–4in) apart in groups. After flowering let foliage die down naturally. Divide overgrown clumps occasionally in summer or autumn.
Propagation:	Divide in summer or autumn.
Recommended:	C. ancyrensis or 'Golden Bunch'; C. angustifolius (Cloth of Gold) and 'Minor'; C. tommasinianus, sold in mixtures and single colours (albus, 'Barrs Purple', 'Lilac Beauty', 'Ruby Giant').
Useful tip:	Do not mow until the foliage of plants grown in grass has died down.
Related plants:	Autumn-flowering C. laevigatus can continue into winter.

CROCUS TOMMASINIANUS

These dainty early crocuses appear with hardy cyclamen and snowdrops, just as the last aconites are fading, and they are true heralds of the end of winter. The large hybrids that follow after several of the smaller species have finished are very much spring flowers.

CUPRESSUS MACROCARPA 'GOLDCREST'

These beautiful fast-growing trees deserve to be grown in prominent positions as garden features and container shrubs. The feathery foliage of the various golden forms always looks sunny and cheerful, adding a hint of Mediterranean warmth to winter.

Plant type:	Evergreen conifer.
Height:	3–4.5m (10–15ft) if clipped; otherwise 9m (30ft) or more.
Spread:	Up to 3m (10ft).
Soil:	Most soils, especially lighter ones; avoid very wet ground.
Positioning:	Full sun with shelter from cold winds. Ideal for windbreaks in coastal areas. Grow as specimens in lawns and borders, or 90cm (3ft) apart as hedging.
Planting time:	Mid-spring.
Care:	Plant pot-grown specimens at 45–60cm (18–24in) high and shelter from cold winds while young. Trim every mid-spring without cutting into old wood.
Propagation:	Grow cuttings in a cold frame in autumn.
Recommended:	'Donard Gold' (conical), 'Goldcrest' (slim tree), 'Gold Spread' (prostrate).
Useful tip:	Named cultivars may be difficult to root as cuttings, so take plenty to allow for losses.
Related plants:	*C. sempervirens* (Italian Cypress); best forms 'Green Pencil' and 'Swanes Golden'.

Cyclamen coum Hardy Cyclamen

Plant type: Deciduous corm.
Height: 8cm (3in).
Spread: 15cm (6in).
Soil: Well-drained; humus.
Positioning: Dappled sunlight or semi-shade, in drifts under deciduous trees (in short grass) and shrubs; at the front of beds, in rock gardens and containers. Grow with winter aconites and snowdrops.
Planting time: Dry corms in spring; pot-grown plants any time.
Care: Plant 15–20cm (6–8in) apart, 5cm (2in deep) in groups. Mulch in early autumn with compost or composted bark. Mow plants in grass in early summer and leave clippings for a few days for ripe seeds to shed.
Propagation: Sow ripe seeds in pots or scatter in situ.
Recommended: Normal species; also ssp. *coum album*, 'Atkinsii', 'Maurice Dryden', 'Roseum' and the Pewter-leafed Group.
Useful tip: Undisturbed plants will set seeds freely.
Related plants: *C. repandum*.

CYCLAMEN COUM

These dainty early-flowering plants are totally hardy and prolific where there is good drainage. They have a unique charm and delicacy as their upswept, rather exotic, blooms unfurl from mid-winter onwards. They vary from white to rich pink, and the rounded leaves are often prettily marbled.

DAPHNE ODORA 'AUREOMARGINATA'

Both deciduous *D. mezereum* (Mezereon) and evergreen *D. odora* (Winter Daphne) are renowned for the fragrance of their tiny white, pink or red blooms which are produced in dense clusters from mid-winter onwards. On still days the perfume hangs in the air. All parts of the plants are poisonous.

Plant type: Deciduous and evergreen shrubs.

Height: 1.2m (4ft).

Spread: 90cm (3ft).

Soil: Fertile, not too chalky; moist but well-drained.

Positioning: Dappled sunlight or semi-shade, with some protection from cold winds. Grow beside paths and gates, at the front of borders, in containers.

Planting time: Autumn or spring.

Care: Mulch with compost after planting and then every spring; water in dry seasons. Protect evergreen forms from cold winds. Spray against aphids in summer if necessary.

Propagation: Sow species seeds under glass in spring; grow cuttings in a cold frame in summer.

Recommended: *D. mezereum*; also *alba and* var. *rubra.* *D. odora*; also *alba*, *rubra*, and 'Aureomarginata' and 'Walburton' (both variegated).

Useful tip: Chalky soils cause yellow leaves – treat with sequestered iron.

Related plants: *D. bholua*, deciduous or evergreen.

Elaeagnus (evergreen) Oleaster

Plant type: Evergreen shrub.
Height: 3m (10ft).
Spread: 3m (10ft).
Soil: Fertile, well-drained; avoid shallow chalk.
Positioning: Full sun for best colour, light shade tolerated. Grow green forms behind deciduous winter-flowering plants, variegated kinds as specimen and wall-trained shrubs. Plant 45–60cm (18–24in) apart for hedging.
Planting time: Autumn or spring.
Care: Mulch with compost in spring. Prune to shape in mid-spring; clip hedges in early summer and autumn.
Propagation: Grow cuttings under glass in summer.
Recommended: E. pungens 'Dicksonii' (gold edges), 'Frederici' (pale cream, green edges), 'Maculata' (yellow centres), 'Variegata' (cream edges); E. × ebbingei (silver/grey-green leaves); also 'Limelight' (gold splashes), 'Gilt Edge'.
Useful tip: In very cold gardens, variegated leaves may be scorched by winds.
Related plants: E. macrophylla.

ELAEAGNUS × EBBINGEI 'LIMELIGHT'

Oleasters are some of the best evergreen shrubs for all-year-round beauty, tough enough to withstand most inland winters and salt- and wind-resistant for seaside gardens. Bright variegated forms catch the winter sunlight. The early spring flowers are creamy white and very fragrant.

ERANTHIS HYEMALIS 'GUINEA GOLD'

The first sign of reviving life in mid-winter is the appearance of winter aconites. The bright 'buttercups', which open almost flat in full sun, are enclosed by ruffs of green leaves, but the main foliage develops after the blooms fade. Seeds ripen mid- to late spring, and are dispersed freely around the plants which soon develop into natural clumps and drifts without being invasive.

Plant type: Herbaceous tuber.

Height: 5–8cm (2–3in).

Spread: 8cm (3in).

Soil: Most well-drained soils.

Positioning: Dappled sunlight or light shade, beneath shrubs and deciduous trees. Naturalize at the edge of borders and paths, in short grass and rock gardens. Grow with crocuses and hardy cyclamen.

Planting time: Dried tubers in early autumn, 'in the green' in late spring.

Care: Plant 5cm (2in) deep and 15–20cm (6–8in) apart in groups or drifts. Water occasionally in dry springs, mulch in summer with compost or composted bark.

Propagation: Divide immediately after flowering; scatter ripe seeds in situ or sow in a cold frame.

Recommended: Basic species; also double 'Flore Pleno' and 'Guinea Gold'.

Useful tip: Plants are more suited to natural planting than formal schemes in flower beds.

Related plants: None.

Plant type: Dwarf evergreen shrub.

Height: 15–90cm (6–36in).

Spread: 45–90cm (18–36in).

Soil: All moist but well-drained soils; avoid very chalky sites.

Positioning: Full sun or very light shade only; in small groups or as edging; also in pots and window boxes. Plant 30–38cm (12–15in) apart in drifts for ground cover.

Planting time: Autumn.

Care: Mulch with compost in spring. Prune after blooms fade; trim flowering shoots with shears and cut out straggly shoots.

Propagation: Grow cuttings from side-shoots in a cold frame in summer.

Recommended: *E. carnea* 'December Red', 'Golden Starlet', 'Springwood White', 'Westwood Yellow'; *E. × darleyensis* 'Arthur Johnson' (syn. 'Dunwood Splendour'), 'Jack H. Brummage', 'White Perfection'.

Useful tip: Grow with dwarf conifers or rosemary for winter schemes.

Related plants: *Calluna vulgaris* (see page 18).

ERICA × DARLEYENSIS 'DUNWOOD SPLENDOUR'

Although some heathers need acid soils, the most popular kinds are the reliably lime-tolerant ones. There are many winter-flowering varieties of these. They all provide excellent flower and foliage colour, and thrive in the harshest conditions as shrubs, ground cover or winter container plants.

Eucalyptus gunnii Cider Gum

EUCALYPTUS GUNNII

This is one of the hardiest eucalypts, and its round, silver-blue young leaves and the multicoloured peeling bark on older trees make it possibly the most popular. Growth continues throughout the year, so young foliage is susceptible to savage frosts – but most years plants survive unscathed.

Plant type:	Evergreen tree.
Height:	Up to 30m (100ft), usually much smaller.
Spread:	3m (10ft) or more.
Soil:	Most if well-drained.
Positioning:	Full sun with shelter from cold winds, as a specimen in lawns and shrubberies, grouped as a grove. Grow as a bush in a container if space is limited.
Planting time:	Early summer as pot-grown plants.
Care:	For a tree, cut down to 30cm (12in) after planting and grow the strongest new stem. Leave all stems to form a bush. In severe winters cover young plants with fleece. Prune one-third of branches each spring for young foliage.
Propagation:	Sow seeds indoors in warmth in spring.
Recommended:	Basic species only.
Useful tip:	Cut the young foliage at any time for flower arrangements.
Related plants:	E. dalrympleana (Mountain Gum); E. glaucescens (Tingiringi Gum); E. pauciflora ssp. niphophila (Snow Gum).

Euonymus fortunei / Evergreen Euonymus

Plant type: Evergreen shrub.

Height: Bush 90cm (3ft), wall-trained 3m (10ft).

Spread: 2–3m (6½–10ft).

Soil: Most fertile, well-drained soils.

Positioning: Full sun or very light shade for best colours, semi-shade for green forms; as specimen shrubs, ground cover, backdrop for summer flowers. Grow 30–38cm (12–15in) apart for hedging.

Planting time: Autumn or spring.

Care: After planting cut back growth by one-third. Trim bushes annually in spring, hedges in spring or mid-summer.

Propagation: Grow cuttings under glass in summer, in a cold frame in winter.

Recommended: 'Blondy', 'Emerald 'n Gold', 'Emerald Gaiety', 'Silver Queen', 'Sun Spot'.

Useful tip: Grow the above varieties as container shrubs or simple topiary.

Related plants: E. japonicus, basic green forms; also variegated 'Aureus', 'Duc d'Anjou', 'Ovalus Aureus', 'Latifolius Albomarginatus'.

EUONYMUS FORTUNEI 'EMERALD GAIETY'

These tough, self-reliant shrubs brighten any gloomy corner and are also excellent for training on a wall, where the branches will develop aerial roots. Plants tolerate dry soils, urban pollution and sea spray, making them ideal for challenging positions.

Euphorbia characias
Spurge, Milkweed

EUPHORBIA CHARACIAS

Although most often chosen for their dramatic spring-flowering heads of brightly coloured bracts, varieties also make clumps of handsome evergreen stems that guarantee winter colour. Plants are happy in most garden situations.

Plant type: Evergreen perennial.
Height: 90cm (36in).
Spread: 90cm (36in).
Soil: Well-drained, fertile.
Positioning: Full sun or light shade, with some shelter from cold winds; singly or in small groups in beds and borders, also in containers. Ideal on corners, flanking a gateway.
Planting time: Spring or autumn.
Care: Undemanding once established. Mature plants resent being moved. Mulch with compost in spring; cut down every few years in spring.
Propagation: Divide in autumn or spring; sow seeds in a cold frame in spring.
Recommended: Normal species; also ssp. *characias* (purple-centred flowers); ssp. *wulfenii* (yellow centres), 'John Tomlinson' (gold flowers), 'Variegata' (cream-edged leaves).
Useful tip: The milky sap can irritate the skin.
Related plants: Good winter plants include *E. polychroma*, *E. robbiae*, variegated *E. wallichii*.

Fatsia japonica Japanese Aralia

Plant type: Evergreen shrub.
Height: Up to 3m (10ft).
Spread: 3–3.7m (10–12ft).
Soil: Rich; moist but not waterlogged.
Positioning: Light to semi-shade, with shelter from cold winds. Ideal for shady corners, warm walls, coastal gardens, as a specimen or behind other evergreens.
Planting time: Late spring. Harden off thoroughly before planting out if bought as a houseplant.
Care: Feed every spring with a general fertilizer; water regularly in dry summers. Mulch in autumn with compost. Leave unpruned or remove a few branches and shorten others in late spring.
Propagation: Grow cuttings indoors in summer.
Recommended: Normal species; also 'Variegata'.
Useful tip: Regular watering and feeding helps produce the largest leaves.
Related plants: *Tetrapanax papyrifer* (formerly *Fatsia papyrifera*), shrub for winter containers in conservatories.

FATSIA JAPONICA

The glossy palm-shaped leaves of this dense shrub are very large, especially in moist soils, and add a subtropical atmosphere to sheltered corners and courtyards. The long-lasting cream flower spikes appear in mid-autumn and are followed by large clusters of black fruits that ripen the following spring.

Galanthus Snowdrop

GALANTHUS ELWESII

Snowdrops are virtually indestructible, and survive the harshest weather. No amount of snow or frost prevents their welcome appearance in mid- and late winter. They complement golden winter aconites and fade only as the spring crocus season gets under way. There are many different varieties, all desirable.

Plant type: Herbaceous bulb.
Height: 15–23cm (6–9in).
Spread: 15cm (6in).
Soil: Most kinds; moist, fertile soils preferred.
Positioning: Full sun for the earliest blooms, light shade to prolong flowering; in groups and drifts under trees, shrubs and hedges, in short grass and containers. Naturalize in gloomy corners, wild gardens.
Planting time: Dried bulbs in early autumn; 'in the green' in late spring.
Care: Mulch with leaf mould, compost or composted bark in autumn; top-dress in spring with bonemeal. Let leaves die down naturally. Divide congested clumps every few years.
Propagation: Divide after flowering; replant at once; sow seeds in pots in a cold frame or scatter in situ.
Recommended: Basic species; also double 'Flore Pleno', 'Ophelia' and 'Pusey Green Tip'.
Useful tip: Prepare soil thoroughly, especially if planting dry bulbs.
Related plants: G. elwesii.

Garrya elliptica (Silk) Tassel Bush

GARRYA ELLIPTICA

Plant type: Evergreen shrub.
Height: 4m (13ft).
Spread: 3m (10ft).
Soil: Most kinds.
Positioning: Full sun or semi-shade, with some shelter at flowering time. Best against a warm or shaded wall to keep plants neat and provide protection from wind-scorch. Tolerates pollution, sea spray.
Planting time: Early autumn or spring.
Care: Undemanding, but plants resent being moved. Trim lightly to shape after flowering and remove up to one-third of older branches to maintain size.
Propagation: Grow cuttings under glass in summer, in a cold frame in autumn.
Recommended: Basic species, male or female forms; also 'James Roof' a vigorous male with catkins 30cm (12in) or more in length.
Useful tip: Where there is room, leave bushes unpruned except for the removal of dead wood.
Related plants: *G.* × *isaquahensis*, especially 'Pat Ballard'.

In winter the familiar male form of this shrub displays long, silvery grey tassels that look conspicuous against its sombre olive-green foliage. The less common female plants are decorative too, with crops of purple-brown fruits in summer.

Gaultheria Partridge Berry

GAULTHERIA 'SIGNAL'

These evergreen shrubs are perfect companions for rhododendrons and other ericaceous plants. Some forms are large bushes, others low ground-cover plants. All have dense attractive winter foliage in tints that sometimes complement the lingering brightly coloured berries. Many of the prostrate and dwarfer shrubby species are ideal for alpine sinks and rock gardens, where they make tight mats of neat foliage, sometimes only 5cm (2in) high.

Plant type:	Evergreen shrub.
Height:	1.5m (5ft), often less.
Spread:	1.5–3m (5–10ft).
Soil:	Moist, with humus; acid.
Positioning:	Light or semi-shade; as specimens under deciduous trees or in shrubberies. Plants spread by underground runners and make effective ground cover.
Planting time:	Autumn or spring.
Care:	Undemanding in the right soil. Mulch with leaf mould in spring. Prune dead or straggly stems in spring and cut suckers and creeping roots with a spade.
Propagation:	Grow cuttings in a cold frame in summer; layer stems in spring.
Recommended:	*G. mucronata* (syn. *Pernettya mucronata*), many female varieties; *G. procumbens*, prostrate with reddish foliage; *G. shallon*, green foliage.
Useful tip:	Plant in groups of three including a male such as *G. m.* 'Thymifolia', for good berries.
Related plants:	*G × wisleyensis* (syn. × *Gaulnettya*) 'Wisley Pearl'.

Plant type: Evergreen shrub, small tree.

Height: 4m (13ft), more in mild gardens.

Spread: 3m (10ft) or more.

Soil: Most kinds, if free-draining; avoid very alkaline conditions.

Positioning: Full sun or light shade, protected from cold winds. Best in coastal and sheltered city sites, as specimens in borders, containers; plant 60–90cm (2–3ft) apart as an internal hedge.

Planting time: Mid-spring.

Care: Screen plants until established. Feed with general fertilizer in spring, mulch with compost in autumn and protect inland plants with fleece over winter. Trim after planting; clip or prune in late spring or late summer.

Propagation: Grow cuttings in heat in summer, in a cold frame in mid-autumn.

Recommended: Normal species; also 'Dixons Cream', 'Bantry Bay', 'Variegata'.

Useful tip: Cut out green shoots from variegated forms.

Related plants: None.

GRISELINIA LITTORALIS 'VARIEGATA'

Griselinia is a popular evergreen for seaside gardens, where it can produce a tough hedge or large free-standing trees with dense fresh-looking foliage. Elsewhere plants, especially variegated kinds, can be grown in large containers for bright, eye-catching colour all winter.

Hamamelis mollis ^{Chinese Witch Hazel}

HAMAMELIS MOLLIS 'PALLIDA'

Witch hazels look enchanting against a dark evergreen background or the clear blue winter sky, with their bare branches smothered in ragged fragrant flowers. Plants are tough and frost-proof, with the bonus of vivid yellow or crimson leaf tints in autumn.

Plant type: Deciduous shrub, small tree.

Height: 3–3.5m (10–11½ft).

Spread: 4m (13ft).

Soil: Most well-drained soils, except very alkaline ones.

Positioning: Full sun or light shade, in a mixed border or wild garden. Add herbaceous perennials or a companion clematis for summer interest.

Planting time: Autumn or spring.

Care: Water well in dry weather; mulch with compost in autumn and late spring. Prune lightly to shape in spring and remove dead or diseased wood.

Propagation: Varieties are normally budded in summer or grafted in winter on *H. virginiana* rootstocks; cuttings under glass in summer can be successful.

Recommended: 'Brevipetala', 'Pallida', 'Sandra'.

Useful tip: Do not prune too hard back into old wood.

Related plants: *H. × intermedia* hybrids with good winter flowers include 'Diane', 'Moonlight' and 'Sunburst'.

Hebe / Veronica

Plant type: Evergreen shrub.

Height: 60cm–1.5m (2–5ft).

Spread: 45cm–1.5m (18in–5ft).

Soil: Any moist fertile soil unless waterlogged.

Positioning: Full sun or very light shade, protected from cold winds. Grow dwarf kinds as edging, ground cover or in a rock garden; taller varieties as specimens, hedges, in containers.

Planting time: Spring; autumn in mild gardens.

Care: Plant slightly tender varieties deeply. Water the shallow roots in dry seasons. Trim after flowering.

Propagation: Grow cuttings under glass in late spring, in a cold frame in autumn.

Recommended: Dwarf: *H. albicans*; *H. pinguifolia* 'Pagei'; *H.* 'Red Edge'. Tall: *H.* × *franciscana* 'Blue Gem' and 'Variegata'; *H. ochracea* 'James Stirling'; *H. armstrongii*.

Useful tip: Remove green shoots from variegated kinds.

Related plants: Many tender varieties for containers and conservatories.

HEBE 'RED EDGE'

Hebes come in a huge range of sizes, shapes and colours, but all are lovely evergreens, with dense immaculate foliage that, sadly, is not always frost-hardy. Most are sound choices for seaside gardens. Those listed here are reliable winter shrubs for inland areas.

HEDERA HELIX 'TRILOBA'

Plant type:	Evergreen climber, shrub.
Height:	90cm–5m (3–15ft) or more.
Spread:	1.2–3m (4–10ft).
Soil:	Most, except very acid kinds.
Positioning:	Full sun or light shade for variegated kinds, deeper shade for green varieties. Grow erect shrubby forms as shrubs, in rock gardens. Use climbers for ground cover and on fences and sound walls.
Planting time:	Autumn or spring.
Care:	Plants may need a year to settle in to a new site. Trim back over-vigorous growth.
Propagation:	Grow cuttings in a cold frame in summer; layer in autumn.
Recommended:	'Atropurpurea', 'Buttercup', 'Glacier', 'Glymii', 'Marginata', 'Tricolor'.
Useful tip:	Plant non-climbing forms like 'Congesta', 'Conglomerata' and 'Erecta' 38–45cm (15–18in) apart for excellent hedges.
Related plants:	*H. hibernica* 'Gracilis'; also 'Anne Marie' and 'Maculata'.

Ivies are a remarkable group of plants. Some with vigorous self-clinging climbers, often with brilliantly variegated foliage; other varieties are stiff non-climbing woody shrubs that make unusual hedges and bushes. All provide excellent winter colour, often with crops of berries that are coveted by hungry birds.

Helichrysum italicum Curry Plant

Plant type: Evergreen shrub.
Height: 60cm (2ft).
Spread: 30–45cm (12–18in).
Soil: Warm, light, well-drained; not too fertile.
Positioning: Full sun, with shelter from cold winds, late frosts; as specimens in herb gardens and beside paths or 23cm (9in) apart as a decorative hedge. Combine with thymes and helianthemums.
Planting time: Autumn or spring.
Care: Mulch in spring with composted bark. Trim to shape in spring, and shear off flowers from formal plantings. Take cuttings as insurance or screen from hard frosts.
Propagation: Grow cuttings under glass in summer.
Recommended: Basic species; dwarf ssp. *microphyllum* and 'Nanum'. Also *H. petiolare*, especially 'Limelight' (gold) and 'Variegatum' (light and dark grey); *H. plicatum* (silver grey); *H. splendidum* (greyish-white).
Useful tip: Overgrown plants can be cut hard in spring.
Related plants: *Ozothamnus* varieties are very similar.

HELICHRYSUM ITALICUM

These grey and silver plants are always welcome in winter, especially on light soils where there is no risk of waterlogging. They are less glamorous than some other shrubs, but their softly rounded shapes and aromatic foliage are reminiscent of warmer climates. (syns. *H. angustifolium, H. serotinum*.)

HELLEBORUS ARGUTIFOLIUS

Hellebores are some of the most valuable plants for the winter garden. Early-flowering and totally weatherproof, they come in a range of gorgeous or reticent colours. They are long-lived, easy to raise and grow, and adapt readily to most situations.

Plant type: Evergreen or semi-evergreen perennial.

Height: 45–60cm (18–24in).

Spread: 60cm (24in).

Soil: Fertile; moist but well-drained; humus.

Positioning: Dappled sunlight or semi-shade; some varieties under trees, others in more open positions in shaded corners; at the edge of shrubberies. Grow singly or in groups.

Planting time: Autumn or spring.

Care: Mulch with very well-rotted manure after flowering; or mulch with leaf mould or compost and feed with bonemeal.

Propagation: Sow seeds in a cold frame in autumn; divide in autumn or spring.

Recommended: *H. argutifolius* (syn. *H. corsicus*), apple-green flowers; *H. foetidus*, creamy green flowers; *H. niger* (Christmas Rose), white flowers; *H. orientalis* (Lenten Rose), white, pink or purple shades.

Useful tip: Plants cross-breed and set plenty of seed, always worth sowing.

Related plants: None.

Plant type: Evergreen perennial.
Height: 45–60cm (18–24in).
Spread: 38–50cm (15–20in).
Soil: Fertile; moist but well-drained; preferably slightly acid.
Positioning: Full sun or very light shade; in groups at the edge of borders, beds, and in containers. Grow with hardy geraniums, heathers, polemoniums, pansies.
Planting time: Autumn or spring.
Care: Fertilize in spring and mulch with compost or composted bark. Divide every 4–5 years.
Propagation: Divide in spring.
Recommended: H. americana (green leaves with orange-copper shading); H. cylindra 'Greenfinch' (silvery green with chocolate veins); H. micrantha, var. diversifolia 'Palace Purple' (papery plum-purple foliage); H. sanguinea (dark green marbled leaves).
Useful tip: If frost heaves plants from the ground, divide and replant or mound soil around stems.
Related plants: x Heucherella tiarelloides.

HEUCHERA 'PALACE PURPLE'

Although they are usually grown for their graceful panicles of white, pink or red flowers, Heuchera are also worth planting for their foliage alone. The fat clumps of tinted leaves, sometimes with pretty markings, persist all winter.

43

Ilex Holly

ILEX CORNUTA 'BURFORDII'

There are hundreds of fine hollies, all of them robust and wind-resistant in any situation. They can be pruned as specimen shrubs, topiary and container plants, especially variegated female varieties whose leaves and berries provide reliable winter colour.

Plant type: Evergreen shrub, tree.

Height: Up to 8m (26ft).

Spread: 3m (10ft).

Soil: Most if well-drained.

Positioning: Sun or shade; best in indirect light but heavy shade reduces fruiting and leaf variegation. Tolerates city air and salt spray. Grow as specimens or plant 60–90cm (2–3ft) apart as a hedge. Ideal backdrop for flower borders.

Planting time: Autumn or spring.

Care: Undemanding when established. Mulch young plants with compost in spring. Clip specimens to shape in late spring; trim hedges in late summer or hard prune in mid-spring. Cut out green shoots from variegated plants.

Propagation: Grow cuttings in a cold frame in autumn.

Recommended: I. × altaclarensis 'Lawsoniana'; I. aquifolium 'Handsworth New Silver'; I. cornuta 'Burfordii'; I. crenata 'Golden Gem'.

Useful tip: Plants may shed leaves in their first year.

Related plants: None.

Iris foetidissima Gladwyn, Gladdon

Plant type: Evergreen perennial.
Height: 60cm (24in).
Spread: 45cm (18in).
Soil: Moist, fertile; a little lime.
Positioning: Semi- or light shade with some shelter from wind. Ideal in shaded corners, wild gardens and under deciduous trees. Grows well beneath a shaded wall, with ferns and hellebores.
Planting time: Late summer.
Care: Plant rhizomes 30cm (12in) apart at, or just below, the soil surface. Cut down old foliage as new leaves appear.
Propagation: Sow seeds in a cold frame or in situ in autumn; divide immediately after flowering.
Recommended: Basic species; also var. *citrina* (larger leaves, flowers pale yellow), 'Variegata' (cream-striped leaves), 'Fructu Albo' (white seeds).
Useful tip: Flowers and seedheads are good for cutting.
Related plants: *I. pallida* and forms 'Variegata' and 'Argentea Variegata'.

IRIS FOETIDISSIMA

Although the early summer flowers are not the most spectacular, they are followed by bizarre seedheads which crack open to reveal bright orange seeds that persist for months. Forms with striped foliage are the only reliably evergreen variegated irises, and colour best in heavy shade.

IRIS RETICULATA 'IDA'

These dwarf irises are called *Iris reticulata* because their bulbs are covered with a fine net of fibres. The plants sometimes appear as early as mid-winter, when their dainty blooms, often extravagantly marked, provide rich colour for the garden. The many hybrids are often the result of crosses with larger-flowered *I. histrioides*.

Plant type: Perennial bulb.

Height: 15cm (6in).

Spread: 8–10cm (3–4in).

Soil: Any well-drained soil.

Positioning: Full sun for early flowers; plants tolerate some shade. Group as bold patches at the front of borders, in rock gardens; also in containers and short grass. Grow with snowdrops and hardy cyclamen.

Planting time: Early to late autumn.

Care: Plant 8–10cm (3–4in) apart and 8–10cm (3–4in) deep in groups. Cover with sharp sand on clay.

Propagation: Divide clumps in autumn; replant immature bulblets or line them out in spare ground until they reach flowering size.

Recommended: Basic deep blue species; also mixed seedlings, named forms such as 'Alba' (white), 'Cantab' (pale blue), 'Joyce' (lavender), 'Royal Blue', 'Violet Beauty'.

Useful tip: Let leaves die down naturally, especially where grown in grass.

Related plants: *I. danfordiae*.

Plant type: Evergreen perennial.
Height: 38cm (15in).
Spread: 38–45cm (15–18in).
Soil: Fertile, free draining; dry in summer, moist in winter.
Positioning: Hot, dry, sunny; ideally below a wall. Eventually makes large clumps for narrow beds and borders, in dry and paved areas.
Planting time: Autumn or spring.
Care: Mulch lightly with dried manure in spring or feed annually with general fertilizer. Remove dead leaves after flowering. Divide mature clumps every 5–6 years.
Propagation: Divide after flowering.
Recommended: Basic species; also many cultivated forms including *alba*, 'Mary Barnard' (violet blue), 'Marginata' (lilac and white), 'Oxford Dwarf' (deep blue, compact), 'Walter Butt' (ice-blue).
Useful tip: May be reluctant to flower unless the position is ideal.
Related plants: *I. cretica*, now thought to be *I. unguicularis* ssp. *cretensis*.

IRIS UNGUICULARIS 'MARY BARNARD'

In early winter, just when you think no iris would dream of flowering, sharp blue-tipped buds start to appear well down among the foliage. They unfurl into extravagantly marked but short-lived silky blooms. Cut them while still in bud for vases indoors as others will continue to appear steadily until early spring. (syn. *I. stylosa*.)

Juniperus Juniper

JUNIPERUS SQUAMATA 'BLUE STAR'

Low-growing junipers are winter highlights in rock gardens, sinks and other containers, where their dense, almost heather-like, foliage is attractive in all weathers. They are some of the best conifers for chalky soils and retain their bright colours in any situation.

Plant type:	Evergreen conifer.
Height:	Dwarf kinds up to 90cm (3ft).
Spread:	60cm–1.5m (2–5ft).
Soil:	Any well-drained soil.
Positioning:	Full sun or very light shade; as ground cover at the front of borders or in rock gardens. Also in alpine sinks and as specimens in containers, with dwarf bulbs and heathers.
Planting time:	Autumn or spring.
Care:	Mulch in spring with composted bark. Trim to shape if necessary in late summer.
Propagation:	Grow cuttings of side-shoots in a cold frame in autumn.
Recommended:	*J. communis* 'Depressa Aurea', 'Golden Showers'; *J. horizontalis* 'Prince of Wales'; *J. × media* 'Carberry Gold', 'Old Gold'; *J. squamata* 'Blue Carpet', 'Blue Star'; *J. virginiana* 'Grey Owl'.
Useful tip:	Grow blue forms in full sun, golden varieties in very light shade.
Related plants:	Many full-size junipers provide exciting winter colour and form.

Plant type: Herbaceous bulb.
Height: 20–30cm (8–12in).
Spread: 20–30cm (8–12in).
Soil: Any moist fertile soil.
Positioning: Full sun or light shade; in groups or drifts in borders or short grass; also beside water. Grow with crocus varieties like *C. sieberi* 'Albus' which flower at the same time.
Planting time: Autumn; just after flowering.
Care: Plant 15–20cm (6–8in) apart and 8–10cm (3–4in) deep in groups. Feed with bonemeal after flowering.
Propagation: Divide mature clumps when the foliage has died down; sow ripe seeds in a cold frame or scatter them in situ.
Recommended: Basic species; also var. *carpathicum* (yellow markings on petals), var. *vagneri* (two flowers per stem).
Useful tip: Let foliage die down naturally, especially before mowing turf where bulbs are naturalized.
Related plants: *L. trichophyllum*, slightly tender species, ideal for pots under glass.

LEUCOJUM VERNUM

These charming clump-forming bulbs have the largest flowers of all the snowflakes. They resemble those of snowdrops, except that the petals are all the same length whereas the three outer snowdrop petals are much longer than the rest. They are indispensable hardy plants for almost any soil.

Leucothoe fontanesiana Drooping Laurel

LEUCOTHOE FONTANESIANA 'RAINBOW'

If your soil is neutral or acid, this elegant shrub will introduce colour into the garden. Green varieties have red tints at any time but these intensify as temperatures cool. 'Rainbow' is dramatically multicoloured all year round. The clusters of drooping white flowers in spring are a bonus.

Plant type:	Evergreen shrub.
Height:	1.5m (5ft).
Spread:	2m (6½ft).
Soil:	Acid; fertile, moist; not too light.
Positioning:	Semi-shade as in deciduous woodland. Grow as a specimen or *en masse* as ground cover under trees or in wild gardens.
Planting time:	Autumn or spring.
Care:	Mulch in spring with compost or well-rotted manure. Cut back underground runners with a spade when plants spread too far. Trim mature plants to shape in spring or cut back one-third of older growth to ground level.
Propagation:	Grow cuttings in a cold frame in summer; layer in spring.
Recommended:	Basic species; also 'Rainbow' (cream, yellow and pink), 'Rollissonii', 'Scarletta' (scarlet leaves that turn burgundy red in winter).
Useful tip:	Green or red forms succeed in full shade, 'Rainbow' needs lighter shade.
Related plants:	Other species grown as flowering shrubs.

Ligustrum Privet

Plant type: Evergreen or semi-evergreen shrub.
Height: 4m (13ft).
Spread: 3m (10ft).
Soil: Fertile, well-drained.
Positioning: Full sun or semi-shade; as unpruned specimens in borders or flanking a gate. Clip as topiary or plant 45cm (18in) apart as hedging.
Planting time: Autumn.
Care: Trim plants to one-third their height the first spring. Leave mature plants unpruned or trim once or twice in summer; clip hedges 3–4 times in the growing season.
Propagation: Grow cuttings in a cold frame in summer, outdoors in autumn.
Recommended: *L. lucidum* 'Excelsum Superbum' (green and yellow markings), 'Tricolor' (grey-green, pink, yellow); *L. sinense* 'Variegatum' (grey-green and white), 'Vicaryi' (bronze-purple); *L. ovalifolium* 'Aureum' (gold with green centres).
Useful tip: Privet roots are demanding, so fertilize nearby plants annually.
Related plants: None.

LIGUSTRUM OVALIFOLIUM 'AUREUM'

The golden and variegated forms of common privet are some of the most dependable sources of winter colour. Plants are indifferent to soil conditions, easy to manage and evergreen in all but the coldest gardens.

Lonicera × purpusii Shrubby Honeysuckle

LONICERA × PURPUSII 'WINTER BEAUTY'

Several shrubby honeysuckles are among the cream of winter-flowering bushes. Their delicate long-stamened blooms appear in mid-winter, sometimes earlier, and are all the more conspicuous when borne on bare stems. When cut, their powerful fragrance brings a hint of spring indoors.

Plant type: Deciduous or semi-evergreen shrub.

Height: 1.5m (5ft).

Spread: 1.5m (5ft).

Soil: Fertile; moist but not waterlogged.

Positioning: Full sun for maximum flowers, or light shade; as specimens in borders or shrubberies, or beside paths.

Planting time: Autumn or spring.

Care: Mulch plants in light soils with compost or composted bark in spring. Thin old flowering shoots by one-third after flowering or clip all stems to just beyond the old wood.

Propagation: Grow cuttings under glass in summer, in a cold frame in autumn.

Recommended: Basic species or 'Winter Beauty'.

Useful tip: Combine with a climber such as clematis for later interest.

Related plants: *L. fragrantissima* (evergreen); *L. nitida* 'Baggesens Gold' and 'Silver Beauty' (evergreen dwarf hedging if planted 30cm/12in) apart); *L. setifera; L. standishii.*

Plant type: Evergreen shrub.

Height: 4m (13ft).

Spread: 3.5m (11½ft).

Soil: Fertile, moisture-retentive; avoid shallow chalk.

Positioning: Dappled or semi-shade, with some protection from the coldest winds. Grow as specimens in borders and in positions where their impressive shape can be emphasized.

Planting time: Autumn or spring.

Care: Deadhead young plants after flowering, cutting just below the top leaf rosette; remove wind-scorched foliage and leggy stems in spring.

Propagation: Grow cuttings in summer under glass.

Recommended: 'Charity' is the most widely available; also 'Buckland', 'Lionel Fortescue', 'Underway' (compact), 'Winter Sun'.

Useful tip: The foliage can be scorched by cold winds, so a little shelter is useful.

Related plants: M. japonica.

MAHONIA × MEDIA 'UNDERWAY'

All winter-flowering mahonias are handsome shrubs. Their stout stems carry large impressive leaves, each made up of many spiny leaflets which are often richly tinted in autumn. The clustered branching flower spikes are sweetly scented and borne from autumn to early spring according to variety.

Nandina domestica Sacred Bamboo

NANDINA DOMESTICA 'WOODS DWARF'

This handsome evergreen shrub certainly looks like a bamboo, but it is in fact a member of the berberis family. In addition to fiery winter colour and red berries, plants produce purple-tinted new leaves in spring.

Plant type: Evergreen or semi-evergreen shrub.

Height: Up to 1.5m (5ft).

Spread: 1.2–1.5m (4–5ft).

Soil: Most fertile well-drained soils.

Positioning: Full sun for best colour, sheltered from cold winds. Grow as a specimen among other shrubs, behind herbaceous perennials; also in containers. Plant 45–60cm (18–24in) apart for a low hedge.

Planting time: Autumn or spring.

Care: Mulch with compost in spring. In cold gardens mulch thickly with leaves or straw in autumn and shelter plants from winds. Thin out some old stems in mid-spring.

Propagation: Grow cuttings in a cold frame in summer.

Recommended: Normal species; also 'Firepower' (compact), 'Nana Purpurea' (compact), 'Richmond' (vigorous), 'Woods Dwarf' (compact).

Useful tip: If plants are overgrown or injured by winter weather, cut them to ground level in spring.

Related plants: None.

Plant type: Perennial bulb.

Height: 10–38cm (4–15in).

Spread: 10–15cm (4–6in).

Soil: Any moist leafy soil that is not waterlogged.

Positioning: Full sun or semi-shade, in groups and patches in beds, borders and naturalized in short grass; in containers. Mix with crocuses and primroses.

Planting time: Early autumn.

Care: Plant 15cm (6in) apart and 10cm (4in) deep in groups. Let foliage die down naturally, especially before mowing plants in grass. After flowering top-dress with bonemeal.

Propagation: Sow species seed in a cold frame in summer; divide mature clumps after leaves die down.

Recommended: N. asturiensis; N. cyclamineus; N. romieuxii var. mesatlanticus; also hybrids such as 'Tête-à-Tête', February Gold', 'February Silver' and 'Peeping Tom'.

Useful tip: N. cyclamineus enjoys moist shade and will grow in a bog garden.

Related plants: None.

'FEBRUARY GOLD'

Only a few daffodils earn a place in the winter garden, but they are very choice and welcome. They are all dwarf or miniature forms, with a charm and daintiness all their own: try growing them in pans and other small containers for more intimate enjoyment.

OPHIOPOGON PLANISCAPUS 'NIGRESCENS'

This creeping, clump-forming plant resembles tufts of broad-leafed grass. The most popular and desirable form has purple-black leaves all year, and lilac flowers in summer followed by black fruits. With their darkly mysterious colouring, single plants may be overlooked, whereas bold groups set against a pale background can be an arresting highlight in the winter garden.

Plant type:	Evergreen perennial.
Height:	23cm (9in).
Spread:	30cm (12in).
Soil:	Any fertile, well-drained soil.
Positioning:	Full sun or very light shade, preferably sheltered from the coldest winter winds. Grow in groups at the edge of beds and borders, combined with carpeting plants such as *Ajuga reptans* and dwarf bulbs.
Planting time:	Autumn or spring.
Care:	Water thoroughly from time to time in a dry season; feed occasionally with a general fertilizer. Comb out withered leaves after winter.
Propagation:	Divide clumps in spring.
Recommended:	The dark-leafed form 'Nigrescens' (syns. 'Black Dragon', 'Ebony Knight').
Useful tip:	Plants are particularly effective between paving stones, and as drifts in gravel paths.
Related plants:	*O. intermedius* 'Argenteomarginatus' and *O. japonicus* 'Silver Dragon' are hardier.

Phyllostachys aurea — Fishpole Bamboo

Plant type:	Evergreen bamboo.
Height:	Up to 8m (26ft).
Spread:	1.2m (4ft) or more.
Soil:	Fertile; moist but not waterlogged.
Positioning:	Light shade, tolerates full sun. Grow where plants can eventually form large clumps, at the back of borders, as windbreaks and hedges; as specimen clumps in lawns.
Planting time:	Autumn or spring.
Care:	On very light soils mulch in spring with compost. Clip sides and tops in summer if space is limited. Cut out old canes from mature clumps.
Propagation:	Divide clumps in late spring.
Recommended:	Basic species; also 'Albovariegata' (white striped leaves), 'Holochrysa' (green/yellow striped stems and leaves), 'Variegata' (yellow striped leaves).
Useful tip:	Young shoots are edible; mature stems are valuable for garden canes.
Related plants:	P. bambusoides (Giant Timber bamboo); P. flexuosa.

PHYLLOSTACHYS AUREA

The running roots of many bamboos are too invasive for all except the largest gardens, but most species of Phyllostachys are well-behaved, especially in cooler climates. There are several fine types, among them this graceful species with numerous pretty forms that look intriguing all year.

57

PIERIS JAPONICA 'VARIEGATA'

Although flowering is often in spring, plants deserve space in sheltered winter gardens where conditions are mild and they can start blooming in late winter. Even before opening, the developing flower heads are an attractive pink or red, a feature in themselves.

Plant type: Evergreen shrub.

Height: 1.8m (6ft).

Spread: 1.5m (5ft).

Soil: Acid; leafy and moisture-retentive.

Positioning: Dappled shade, some shelter from cold winds. Grow as specimens in borders, wild gardens and woodland; also in containers. Combine with spring woodland species like primroses and early daffodils.

Planting time: Spring.

Care: Mulch in autumn with compost, leaf mould or composted bark. In late spring, shorten over-vigorous stems and remove frost-damaged shoots by cutting back to uninjured wood.

Propagation: Grow cuttings under glass in summer.

Recommended: 'Christmas Cheer' (very early flowering), 'Dorothy Wyckoff', 'Flamingo', 'Valley Valentine', 'Variegata'.

Useful tip: Plant in containers in alkaline gardens; use ericaceous soil and insulate containers throughout winter.

Related plants: None.

Plant type: Evergreen shrub or small tree.

Height: 6m (20ft).

Spread: 3m (10ft).

Soil: Any well-drained soil.

Positioning: Full sun or light shade; against a warm wall with shelter from cold winds. Can be grown in the open in mild coastal areas, as a specimen or planted 90cm (3ft) apart as a hedge.

Planting time: Early autumn or late spring.

Care: Undemanding if plants are grown in a suitably sheltered position. Trim lightly a year after planting to induce bushy growth. Clip mature plants to shape and cut out winter damage in late spring.

Propagation: Grow cuttings in a propagator in summer.

Recommended: Normal species; also 'Irene Patterson' (pink-white marbling), 'Silver Queen' (grey-green, edged white), 'Tom Thumb' (reddish-purple, dwarf), 'Warnham Gold'.

Useful tip: The foliage is popular for flower-arranging.

Related plants: P. 'Garnettii'.

PITTOSPORUM TENUIFOLIUM 'TOM THUMB'

This is perhaps the hardiest species of a lovely New Zealand race of shrubs. Varieties are mainly grown for their dense distinctive evergreen foliage, which lasts well in water. The tiny spring flowers are an attractive brownish-purple and honey-scented.

PRIMULA VULGARIS SSP. SIBTHORPII

A mild season will often coax a few blooms among the rosettes of fresh new primrose leaves, but this award-winning subspecies is the most reliable for late winter flowers. It is a handsome, unusually coloured form that is a precursor of all the spring flowers soon to follow. For maximum impact, grow separately from ordinary primroses but close enough for these to provide continuity of colour.

Plant type: Herbaceous perennial.

Height: 15cm (6in).

Spread: 30cm (12in).

Soil: Moist loamy soil is best, although other kinds are acceptable.

Positioning: Dappled sunlight or semi-shade; in groups or drifts at the front of borders, beside paths, below hedges; in orchards and short grass, wild gardens. Combine with late snowdrops.

Planting time: Autumn or mid-winter.

Care: Mulch in spring with compost; water in dry seasons. Plant 23–30cm (9–12in) apart in natural patches.

Propagation: Sow seeds in a cold frame in autumn, under glass in spring; divide clumps in spring.

Recommended: Basic subspecies only.

Useful tip: Plants naturalize very readily, and are best grown this way.

Related plants: Other late winter-flowering primulas include *P. amoena*, *P. edgeworthii* (best in a greenhouse or frame), *P. scapigera*, *P. sonchifolia* (best under glass).

Prunus mume Japanese Apricot

Plant type: Deciduous small tree.

Height: Up to 7.5m (25ft).

Spread: 5m (16ft).

Soil: Any kind of soil, provided it contains some lime.

Positioning: Full sun; in mild gardens as a specimen on lawns and in larger shrubberies and paved areas like courtyards; elsewhere on warm walls that are sheltered from cold winds.

Planting time: Autumn or spring.

Care: Stake trees for their first few years and water if their first season is dry. Pruning is seldom necessary and should be done in summer.

Propagation: Grow cuttings in a cold frame in summer.

Recommended: 'Alphandii' (syn. 'Flore Pleno'), 'Pendula', 'Rosemary Clarke', 'Benishidori'.

Useful tip: For large bushes rather than trees, shorten the leading stems in summer.

Related plants: P. subhirtella 'Autumnalis', 'Autumnalis Rosea'; P. serrula.

PRUNUS MUME 'BENISHIDORI'

In favoured gardens, especially where trained against a sunny wall, early varieties of this charming tree are wreathed in fragrant blooms well before any leaves appear. Some forms are more compact than the basic species.

PULMONARIA RUBRA

Lungwort are old-fashioned cottage garden flowers, remarkable in their adaptability and willingness to grow in almost any aspect and soil. This is the earliest flowering species. The blooms first appear in mid-winter and build up to a crescendo in early spring. Unlike other, later-flowering forms, its leaves are usually unspotted. (syn. *P. montana*.)

Plant type: Semi-evergreen perennial.
Height: 30cm (12in).
Spread: 60cm (24in).
Soil: Fertile; moist but well-drained.
Positioning: Dappled sunlight or semi-shade; in groups as edging and ground cover under winter- and spring-flowering shrubs. Combine with snowdrops and miniature daffodils.
Planting time: Autumn or spring.
Care: Mulch with leaf mould or compost in spring; water in dry seasons. Trim old foliage lightly after flowering.
Propagation: Divide mature clumps in autumn or spring, and replant younger portions.
Recommended: Basic species; also *albocorollata* (white flowers), 'Barfield Pink', 'Bowles Red', 'David Ward' (coral flowers).
Useful tip: Do not confuse with *P. officinalis rubra*, a herbal lungwort.
Related plants: *P. saccharata* has spotted leaves all winter, especially 'Mrs. Moon', 'Leopard' and 'Margery Fish'.

Pyracantha Firethorn

Plant type: Evergreen shrub.

Height: 3m (10ft).

Spread: 3m (10ft).

Soil: Any fairly fertile, well-drained soil.

Positioning: Full sun (for berries) or light shade; in most sites including seaside and urban roadside gardens. Grow as a specimen, a mophead topiary standard or on a wall. Plant 60 cm (2ft) apart as hedging.

Planting time: Autumn or spring.

Care: Trim lightly the spring after planting to induce bushy growth. Prune fruiting bushes in late winter: cut back to just beyond old wood.

Propagation: Grow cuttings in a cold frame in summer.

Recommended: Numerous good varieties, including 'Harlequin' (pink and cream variegated leaves), 'Navajo' (orange-red berries), 'Sparkler' (white/pink variegation), 'Orange Glow'.

Useful tip: Tie in wall-trained plants regularly and shorten all new shoots in summer back to the developing berries.

Related plants: Many *Cotoneasters*.

PYRACANTHA 'ORANGE CHARMER'

Pyracanthas brighten up the garden for many weeks from mid-autumn onwards and their masses of vividly coloured berries often survive until late winter. They are versatile plants: their thorny stems are ideal for boundary hedging but are also easily manipulated into ornamental trained shapes.

Rhododendron Rhododendron

RHODODENDRON MUCRONULATUM HYBRID

Rhododendrons are magnificent woodland shrubs, eventually small trees in some cases, that are mostly evergreen and shade-loving. They vary considerably in size and appearance, but all have eye-catching flowers in the first half of the year. Those mentioned here start blooming in mid-winter and continue for several weeks.

Plant type:	Evergreen shrub or small tree.
Height:	1.8–5m (6–15ft) or more.
Spread:	1.8–5m (6–15ft).
Soil:	Generally acid; moist but not waterlogged; fairly fertile.
Positioning:	Dappled sunlight or semi-shade, often with shelter from cold winds; as specimens in shrub borders or massed at the edge of lawns, wild gardens, woodlands. Also in ericaceous compost in containers.
Planting time:	Autumn or spring.
Care:	Mulch in spring with a 5cm (2in) layer of compost, composted bark or leaf mould.
Propagation:	Grow cuttings under glass in summer.
Recommended:	R. mucronulatum (red-purple); R. arboreum (red, white flowers); R. dauricum (purple); R. sutchuenense (pink), 'Nobleanum Venustum' (white and pink), 'Nobleanum Album' (white), 'Nobleanum Roseum'.
Useful tip:	If leaves yellow water with sequestered iron.
Related plants:	None.

Plant type: Deciduous shrub.

Height: 2.4–4m (8–13ft).

Spread: 3–4m (10–13ft).

Soil: Fertile; moist but not waterlogged.

Positioning: Full sun or light shade; in clumps in large shrubberies or wild gardens, or specimen groups backlit by the sun. Allow room for the canes to achieve full size. May be trained against walls.

Planting time: Autumn or spring.

Care: Cut back suckering stems with a spade. Prune all stems to ground level in early spring.

Propagation: Divide or layer in spring.

Recommended: *R. biflorus* (brilliant white hairy stems); *R. cockburnianus* (purple stems with a white bloom); *R. phoenicolasius* (orange-red stems); *R. thibetanus*, especially 'Silver Fern' (brown-purple stems with a white bloom).

Useful tip: Plants grow in the poorest soils.

Related plants: *R. cockburnianus* 'Goldenvale'.

RUBUS COCKBURNIANUS

The strange beauty of these cane-bearing shrubs is undeniable, and a mature stand of white or orange stems in the winter sunlight adds eerie fantasy to the garden. They may be uncomfortable companion plants for other shrubs and really need to be centre-stage for maximum impact.

Ruta graveolens Rue, Herb of Grace

RUTA GRAVEOLENS 'JACKMANS BLUE'

This pungently aromatic herb has been used for centuries for medicinal purposes and is the source of an important essential oil, but its decorative potential is also making it popular as an evergreen ornamental shrub. If pruned annually, the blue-green foliage remains dense and tidy; the mustard-yellow summer flowers may be cut off if not liked.

Plant type: Evergreen shrub.

Height: 75cm (30in).

Spread: 45cm (18in).

Soil: Moist, fertile, well-drained; some lime.

Positioning: Full sun and warmth for the best colouring. Grow as a specimen in herb gardens or at the front of mixed borders; also in groups. Plant 20cm (8in) apart as a low hedge.

Planting time: Spring.

Care: Mulch with compost in autumn and feed with a general fertilizer in spring. Prune to shape and clip hedges in late spring, after frost damage.

Propagation: Sow seeds (species only) in a nursery bed outdoors in spring; grow cuttings in a cold frame in summer.

Recommended: Basic species; also 'Jackmans Blue' and 'Variegata'.

Useful tip: Wear gloves when pruning as plants may cause skin reactions.

Related plants: *R. chalapensis*, slightly tender; best form 'Dimension Two'.

Salix Willow

Plant type: Deciduous shrub, small tree.

Height: 10m (33ft) or more (dwarf) 90cm (3ft).

Spread: 6m (20ft) (dwarf) 1.5m (5ft).

Soil: Most kinds; growth is slow on light sands.

Positioning: Full sun. Grow dwarf forms as specimens in rock and bog gardens, and in containers; others singly or in small groups beside water, in larger borders.

Planting time: Autumn or spring.

Care: Mulch in spring with compost or composted bark and clip shrubby kinds to shape. Cut taller ones almost to the ground in mid-spring.

Propagation: Grow cuttings in late winter in a cold frame or sheltered bed.

Recommended: Dwarf: S. helvetica; S. hastata 'Wehrhahnii' (reddish-purple stems). Tall: S. alba 'Chermesina' (red), 'Vitellina' (yellow); S. daphnoides (purple).

Useful tip: Grow well away from drains, as the roots may penetrate them.

Related plants: S. matsudana 'Tortuosa'.

SALIX ALBA 'VITELLINA'

Willows suitable for growing in gardens may be divided into two kinds: low-growing shrubby types that produce catkins at the end of winter, and taller varieties that are coppiced each year to renew their brightly coloured stems. They are all very easy to grow and tolerant of widely differing conditions.

Salvia officinalis (Common) Sage

SALVIA OFFICINALIS 'ICTERINA'

Although sage is familiar as a robust evergreen herb and essential flavouring in the kitchen, it is less commonly grown as an ornamental shrub. The distinctive foliage gives pleasure all winter, while the richly coloured flowers attract bees in summer. Several other shrubby species may be grown for winter colour if protection from frost can be guaranteed.

Plant type:	Evergreen shrub.
Height:	60cm (24in).
Spread:	75cm (30in).
Soil:	Light, well-drained and fairly fertile, especially for coloured forms.
Positioning:	Full sun, green forms also in light shade, with shelter from cold winter winds. Grow in groups and as specimens in herb gardens, at the front of mixed borders; also 60cm (2ft) apart in rows as edging.
Planting time:	Spring.
Care:	Bury plants up to the lowest branches. Mulch with compost in autumn, feed with a general fertilizer in spring. Trim to shape in late spring.
Propagation:	Grow cuttings under glass in summer.
Recommended:	Basic species; also 'Berggarten' (grey), 'Icterina' (green-yellow edges), Purpurascens Group (greyish-purple) and 'Tricolor' (green, pink and white).
Useful tip:	Coloured sages may die out in winter if they are waterlogged.
Related plants:	*S. elegans* 'Scarlet Pineapple'.

Plant type: Evergreen shrub.

Height: 90cm (3ft), *S. confusa* 1.8m (6ft).

Spread: Up to 1.8m (6ft).

Soil: Most fertile soils, especially chalk.

Positioning: Full sun or semi-shade; as specimens in mixed borders or shrubberies. Also near doorways or in containers to enjoy the perfume.

Planting time: Autumn or spring.

Care: Mulch with compost or well-rotted manure in spring. Trim lightly if needed in late spring, or simply remove dead or damaged wood.

Propagation: Divide in late spring; grow cuttings in a cold frame in autumn.

Recommended: *S. confusa* (creamy flowers); *S. hookeriana*, basic species and also var. *digyna* and more dwarf var. *humilis* (both with pinkish white flowers); *S. orientalis* (upright, vigorous); *S. ruscifolia*, (slow; dark red berries).

Useful tip: Plants may be grown 30cm (12in) apart for dwarf hedging.

Related plants: var. *humilis* 'Purple Stem'.

SARCOCOCCA HOOKERIANA VAR. HUMILIS

Despite their common name, these evergreen shrubs are useless for topiary and seldom need clipping. Apart from the bright glossy foliage, their main winter interest is the powerful sweet fragrance of their flowers, which are small and slightly dishevelled, but pretty nonetheless. These are followed by black or red berries.

SAXIFRAGA 'CORREVONIANA'

Cushion saxifrages are perfectly formed rosette plants that provide winter colour in a rock garden or sink. Leaf margins may be encrusted with lime so that they look frosted. There are hundreds of varieties, most of which flower from late winter onwards. They are very variable in form and attempts have been made to classify them into different sections.

Plant type: Evergreen alpine perennial.

Height: 5–10cm (2–4in).

Spread: 15–30cm (6–12in).

Soil: Light, moist, very well-drained.

Positioning: Dappled sunlight or light shade; in groups as edging to beds and borders, in scree beds and rock gardens. Also in containers like sinks and troughs.

Planting time: Spring.

Care: Mulch generously with gravel or chippings after planting. Grow choice forms in pots, or cover outdoor plants with glass to shield them from prolonged autumn and winter rain.

Propagation: Detach rosettes and plant in a cold frame in early summer.

Recommended: *S. burseriana* 'Gloria' (large white flowers), 'His Majesty' (pink tints), 'Prince Hal' (salmon); *S.* × *kellereri* and *S. Schleicheri* (both pink).

Useful tip: Shield plants grown under glass from the midday sun.

Related plants: *S.* × *urbium* (London Pride); *S. umbrosa*.

Plant type: Herbacious bulb.
Height: 20cm (8in).
Spread: 10cm (4in).
Soil: Most kinds, including heavy ground.
Positioning: Full sun; also beneath deciduous trees. Plant 8cm (3in) deep and 8–10cm (3–4 in) apart in generous groups, especially when naturalized in grass.
Planting time: Autumn.
Care: Feed with a little bonemeal or fertilizer after flowering and let foliage die down naturally; do not mow naturalized groups until mid-summer.
Propagation: Lift bulbs from established groups as leaves die down; separate bulblets and grow in a nursery bed or boxes. Sow seeds in autumn or spring.
Recommended: Basic species; improved form 'Zwanenburg' is sometimes available.
Useful tip: In cold gardens grow in containers to enjoy a very early display.
Related plants: Puschkinia scilloides is very similar but blooms a month later.

SCILLA MISCHTSCHENKOANA

Most squills or wild hyacinths are spring-flowering, but this Caucasian gem is one of the earliest of all 'spring bulbs', often bursting eagerly into bloom in mid-winter on short stems that gradually lengthen. Planted in groups the plants produce a mass of silvery-blue striped stars that almost sparkle in the soft winter sunlight. (syn. *S. tubergeniana*.)

Sedum spathulifolium Stonecrop

SEDUM SPATHULIFOLIUM 'CAPE BLANCO'

Plant type:	Evergreen succulent perennial.
Height:	8–13cm (3–5in).
Spread:	30–45cm (12–18in).
Soil:	Light, very well-drained.
Positioning:	Full sun or light shade; avoid combination of very dry soils and hot sunshine. Grow as ground cover in open gardens, in groups to form carpet edging; also in rock gardens, alpine sinks and troughs and in containers under cover for early flowers.
Planting time:	Autumn or spring.
Care:	Plant 25–30cm (10–12in) apart and mulch with grit or gravel. Remove heavy soil deposits from leaves after storms. Divide and replant every 5–6 years.
Propagation:	Divide in spring.
Recommended:	Basic species; also 'Aureum' (leaves flecked yellow), 'Cape Blanco' (silver-grey), 'Purpureum' (leaves flushed purple).
Useful tip:	Grow where butterflies can graze the flowers.
Related plants:	Many varieties of *S. spurium*.

Most stonecrops (and there are dozens) have interesting evergreen succulent leaves and stems. This North American species is outstanding for its colourful rosettes which soon multiply into tight ground-hugging mats. Surround plants with gravel for dramatic impact and also to keep the foliage unsoiled. Many other sedums are desirable plants, but avoid weedy kinds that tend to be invasive.

Sempervivum tectorum (Common) Houseleek

Plant type: Evergreen succulent perennial.

Height: Up to 15cm (6in).

Spread: 30–45cm (12–18in).

Soil: Light, well-drained, including poor and infertile soils.

Positioning: Full sun with any amount of exposure, in rock gardens, troughs and containers, and as edging to beds and small borders. Also in crevices of paving and walls, even on house roofs.

Planting time: Autumn or spring.

Care: Some species prefer protection from prolonged winter rains. Mulch with grit or gravel after planting.

Propagation: Detach rooted offsets in autumn or spring.

Recommended: Basic species; also 'Atropurpureum', 'Atrorubens', 'Nigrum', 'Atroviolacea', 'Red Flush', 'Royanum' and 'Sunset'.

Useful tip: Flowering rosettes die, but usually leave young offsets at the ends of short runners.

Related plants: S. arachnoideum, especially 'Clairchen' and ssp. tomentosum.

SEMPERVIVUM TECTORUM

There are over a thousand species and varieties of Sempervivum and many gardeners accumulate whole collections of these fascinating and very beautiful summer-flowering succulents. Their symmetrical rosettes of evergreen leaves spread into firm cushions, often finely hairy and delicately coloured. Folk tradition insists that growing these plants on house roofs is a protection against lightning.

SKIMMIA × CONFUSA 'KEW GREEN'

Skimmias are ideal shrubs for any garden, with evergreen foliage, perfumed flowers that open from late winter onwards, and brightly coloured berries that last all autumn and often through winter. They seldom outgrow their positions, and tolerate pollution, shade and seaside conditions.

Plant type: Evergreen shrub.

Height: Up to 1.2m (4ft).

Spread: 90cm–1.2m (3–4ft).

Soil: Moist, fairly fertile; preferably acid.

Positioning: Full sun or semi-shade; as specimens in beds, borders, containers. Female kinds need a male nearby to produce berries. Grow with hellebores and golden evergreen shrubs.

Planting time: Autumn or spring.

Care: Mulch with leaf mould or bark in spring. Deadhead male plants after flowering.

Propagation: Grow cuttings under glass in summer, in a cold frame in autumn.

Recommended: Basic species, and 'Bowles Dwarf' (male or female), 'Nymans' (female), 'Fragrans' (male), ssp. *reevesiana* 'Robert Fortune' (bisexual), 'Rubella' (male), 'Veitchii' (female).

Useful tip: Cut overgrown bushes almost to ground level in spring.

Related plants: S. × *confusa*, best form 'Kew Green' (male); S. *laureola* 'Fragrant Cloud' (bisexual).

Plant type: Evergreen grass.
Height: 1.2–1.5m (4–5ft).
Spread: 60–90cm (2–3ft).
Soil: Rich, fairly dry or well-drained; preferably alkaline.
Positioning: Full sun for the best colouring, with some shelter from strong winds. Display the arching stems to advantage at the top of a bank or wall, in a large container; eye-catching at the front of a border with genista and cytisus.
Planting time: Mid- or late spring.
Care: Mulch lightly with compost in spring. Cut down old foliage as new shoots appear. Divide mature clumps every 4–5 years.
Propagation: Divide in spring.
Recommended: Normal species; also brighter coloured 'Autumn Tints' and 'Gold Hue'; S. calamagrostis and S. gigantea are tall and stately.
Useful tip: Plant as specimens in gravel and among evergreen shrubs, .
Related plants: Calamagrostis × acutiflora.

STIPA ARUNDINACEA

Evergreen grasses are ideal 'designer' plants for the winter garden – their lightness and grace relieves the starkness of bare borders. This is one of the loveliest, with masses of arching feathery flower stems that turn a soft biscuit brown all winter. (syn. *Calamagrostis arundinacea*.)

Trachycarpus fortunei Chusan Palm

TRACHYCARPUS FORTUNEI

Most palms are too frost-shy to grow
successfully anywhere except in extremely
mild districts of Britain, but the Chusan
Palm can withstand moderate frost. In the
right place it will add a tropical air to the
winter garden, whether grown outdoors or
in a container in a conservatory.

Plant type:	Evergreen palm.
Height:	9m (30ft), occasionally more.
Spread:	3–4m (10–13ft).
Soil:	Most, if friable and very well-drained.
Positioning:	Full sun and a warm position, with shelter from strong winds. Often grown as a specimen on lawns or in sunny corners, but better in groups.
Planting time:	Spring.
Care:	Undemanding in the ideal site.
Propagation:	Sow seeds in gritty compost under glass in spring; transplant self-sown seedlings when large enough.
Recommended:	Basic species only.
Useful tip:	In less favoured areas may be grown for several years in a large container with rich gritty compost – bring under glass in winter or move to a frost-free sheltered position.
Related plants:	*T. wagnerianus* (shorter and neater with smaller leaves); *Chamaerops humilis* (the Dwarf Fan Palm), a short palm for mild districts.

Tulipa humilis Tulip

Plant type: Perennial bulb.
Height: 10cm (4in).
Spread: 15–20cm (6–8in).
Soil: Light, well-drained; some lime.
Positioning: Full sun. Plant 10–15cm (4–6in) apart in groups in dry beds or in rock gardens, at the edge of borders; also in containers, outdoors or under glass. Combine with dwarf irises.
Planting time: Late autumn.
Care: Remove fading stems and leaves. Store lifted bulbs in a dry frost-free place until planting time.
Propagation: Remove small offsets when digging up bulbs and replant in autumn in boxes or in rows in a nursery bed.
Recommended: Basic species; also 'Odalisque', 'Persian Pearl', 'Eastern Star' and Violacea Group.
Useful tip: In a late garden, force these varieties in pots under glass; as buds open, harden plants off for a few days for very early blooms outdoors.
Related plants: T. aucheriana is very similar.

TULIPA HUMILIS VAR. PULCHELLA

Only this species of tulip can be relied on to flower before spring, but it is all the more welcome for its readiness to open in the late winter sunshine. It is short-stemmed, like all early tulips, opens very wide and is followed by leaves which lie almost flat on the ground. Bulbs can be left in the ground all year in a warm dry site, or dug up each summer.

Viburnum Viburnum

VIBURNUM TINUS 'LUCIDUM'

There are so many deciduous and evergreen species of Viburnum that it would be easy to have a selection flowering or fruiting all year. Many are valuable winter plants for a number of sites around the garden, and all are tough, reliable and easy to grow.

Plant type: Deciduous and evergreen shrubs.
Height: 90cm–1.8m (3–6ft), sometimes more.
Spread: 90cm–1.8m (3–6ft).
Soil: Fertile, moist.
Positioning: Full sun or light shade, sheltered from winds. Grow as trees and in mixed borders, beside walls and fences, in containers. Plant evergreens 60–90cm (2–3ft) apart as hedges. Grow with winter heathers and spring bulbs.
Planting time: Autumn or spring.
Care: Mulch in spring with compost. Prune to shape in mid-spring; remove a few branches annually from deciduous kinds for an open structure.
Propagation: Grow cuttings under glass in summer, in a cold frame in autumn.
Recommended: Deciduous: V. farreri, V. f. 'Farrer's Pink'; V. × bodnantense, especially 'Dawn'. Evergreen: V. tinus, especially 'Eve Price', 'Gwenllian'.
Useful tip: Grow variegated forms in a warm sunny spot.
Related plants: V. rhytidophyllum.

Plant type: Evergreen biennial or short-lived perennial.

Height: 15–23cm (6–9in).

Spread: 20–23cm (8–9in).

Soil: Fertile; not waterlogged in winter.

Positioning: Full sun or light shade. Plant 23–30cm (9–12in) apart in natural groups and drifts in beds and borders, and as formal bedding. Also in containers, especially hanging baskets.

Planting time: Autumn.

Care: Deadhead flowering stems regularly. Water occasionally in dry seasons and top-dress with general fertilizer in late winter.

Propagation: Sow seeds in summer in a cold frame or outdoors, and thin out or transplant 5–8cm (2–3in) apart.

Recommended: Large-flowered Premiere, Ultima and Universal strains (mixtures and separate colours); small-flowered 'Floral Dance' (mixture and separates).

Useful tip: Root short side-shoots as cuttings in spring.

Related plants: None.

PANSY ULTIMA

Even though there are no truly winter-flowering pansies, these are universally loved and a popular choice for bedding out in autumn. The main display is from early spring onwards, but in an average winter plants will carry a few brightly coloured blooms, especially in a warm corner where they catch the sun.

YUCCA GLORIOSA 'VARIEGATA'

Yucca are magnificent plants, hardier than their tropical appearance might suggest, and worth growing outdoors in favoured positions. They slowly develop into huge evergreen clumps of sword-like foliage that are outstanding in the winter garden. The late summer flowers are strongly fragrant at night.

Plant type: Evergreen shrub.

Height: 1.2–2.4m (4–8ft).

Spread: 1.5m (5ft).

Soil: Light, dry, well-drained.

Positioning: Hot sun, with shelter from cold winds in damp inland areas; ideal for seaside gardens, sandy soils. Grow as specimens in beds, containers or gravel areas; as formal rows flanking paths or drives. Contrast with broadleaf evergreen shrubs.

Planting time: Mid- or late spring.

Care: Remove dying leaves; cut off spent flower stems.

Propagation: Cut off young offsets in spring and root under glass in sand.

Recommended: Normal species; also 'Variegata', with broad yellow edges to the leaves.

Useful tip: Position where the sharp leaf tips and serrated edges cannot injure anyone passing.

Related plants: Y. filamentosa (Adams Needle), best in forms 'Variegata' and 'Bright Edge'.